AF323745

Shift Happens

Dr. Blanche Penn

CONTENTS

Abstract

*You can depend on Pen*n were the words I used when I was running for school board. It is still part of my slogan. Many know me as a mother, grandmother, friend, senior citizen, colleague, freedom fighter, child advocate, volunteer, and pillar of my community. Below, you will find my theme and quotes:

- A child needs direction, and if the direction is clear, the child will succeed.
- Penn is in it to win.
- When you pick up a pen, you will remember me.
- Good morning, good evening, and good night.
- If yesterday was today, and today was yesterday. What would be tomorrow?
- Through the eyes of a child.

My experience in life has been centered on family and having a positive outlook on life. When I was a young child, I needed to understand my strengths and weakness to survive. I have mastered the qualities of being an ethically and spiritually grounded, humble, and diligent worker. Personal development has been a continual process in my life, as it is pertinent to my own, professional, social, and academic goals. I have received these gems of knowledge and added it to my curriculum vitae under the authentic recipe for enhancing my interpersonal skills. The sequence of the ingredients in my recipe is essential because it challenges me to focus my energies in the most productive ways. My preparation begins with a layer of ethics analysis, and then I steam in some transformational learning and sauté the creativity/innovation/inquiry. Also, I needed to understand that things around me will change. The mixture of these ingredients is balanced to perfect the foundation for lifelong learning.

Dedication

This dissertation is dedicated to my beloved husband, Felix Sr., for his unconditional love and support throughout this journey. Thank you for being an exceedingly pleasing husband. It is also dedicated to my children, Rafael, Jasmin, Petronila, and Felix II; and my fourteen grandchildren: Destinee, Malik, Jr., Dre, Makayla, Kobe, and Kyler, Anniah, J'Nair, Stephon, Seyvn, Teigan, Yariah, and K'Mari, and Legend; you all have been unique sources of inspiration during this journey. My love for you all is beyond measure. And now, my grandson, Malik, and my great-granddaughter, Housyton. My parents, Lacy and Helen, and my favorite Aunt Sarah, whom I love so much for believing in me and my goals. You all are uniquely beautiful.

Acknowledgments

God is Good!!! All the Time!!! To God, be the glory!!!

First, God is good, and His love for me to pursue my goals in life was a blessing. I would like to take the time and the opportunity to express my sincere appreciation to the following people and to say thank you from the bottom of my heart. I would also like to thank my editors and all my friends and family who assisted me with my writing. To my family, friends, and the many outstanding community members who worked with me to get through the process of my book, I say thank you. I genuinely appreciate your support, encouragement, and prayers during my work in this book.

Introduction

My professional career was not going anywhere because I did not want to go back to school. I have been married for over 40 years to the love of my life, and we have four children and fourteen grandchildren and one grandchild. I gave up hope and caring about school because I lost so many friends. One night I was out of town, and my sister called me and said to me your mother is in the hospital. I did not get a chance to talk with my mother that day but was on my way home the next day. Before I got back, my mother had passed and the same night more bad news. It was too much to handle at one time. My journey was still moving on a fast track, and it was not turning around to showdown for me. My best friend Valerie said, "Blanche, because of the love and care you have for children, you need to go back to school, and I will help you as much as I can." I was in school, and one night I received a call that she had passed. It was like a train had run off the track, and I was still standing there with my eyes open. Indeed, I was not ready for what happened next. I started back to school because I promise my friend Valerie that I would stay in school. Can you believe that the train did not stop for me it picked up one more passenger, and that person was my husband Felix, and my life turn upside down? Felix and I had two boys, two girls, and many grandchildren. The family has always been important to me. Every holiday, every birthday, even get together, was so unique, and even if I forget them, they will still be in my heart. The events which took place between June 2011 and July of 2011 will never escape my memory. I celebrated my birthday in June, and one of my granddaughters had her sweet 16 Quinceanera in July of 2011. It was so incredibly touching, and looking back, the memory brings heartache as we were not aware that it would be her last party with her grandfather (Papa). Later in July, Felix left for a fishing trip with his best friend Mr. Keith and the neighborhood gang of Century Oaks Lane, since that trip, so much in my life has changed. My children and grandchildren's lives changed, as well.

Nevertheless, we had to move forward. Despite all the grief and pain, we had to move forward because looking back was too hard and painful for us, but memory will live on. God is good and always in control of my life. Working together to move forward was a necessity. I always place family before myself, ensuring they are doing alright. It was like the world was moving, but I was standing in one spot. One night, it saw a shadow came across my bedroom door. I felt my journey was over. All three of my friends and loved ones shared with me to keep going because they said I could do it. I went back to school with a new beginning, a new chapter, and receive my degree in theatre and a master's in education leadership. However, I stayed in school with a challenging program to pursue my Doctor of Education degree and retired in 2017. In the doctorate program, I had to have the time management to maintain at least a 3.0 GPA. I managed a 3.97. I feel my professional career is back on track and going down the right path of life because I have the time and the commitment to finish school with a Doctor of Educational Leadership degree. Now that I have my doctorate this year 2019, it was time for me to sit down and write this book on the authentic recipe of success for anyone that has a goal or goals in mind that they can do it.

The concept of the authentic recipe and the different ingredients needed was my life story. The best person of the epitome of acquired harmonious balance inside and outside of who I am today. They are the nation's greatest assets and the reason why we have esteemed doctors, lawyers, Presidents, and other role models. Many have sacrificed their lives for the sake of their family. I can remember when I was a child; teachers were the backbone of our community. As societal norms change the scope of a leader's responsibility arises with more significant risks. Today, our children are dealing with issues of educational inequality, bullying, obesity, and single parenting. In my experience, while working or volunteering in public schools, I noticed some students have educational gaps in their social and vocabulary skills. It is evident to me why leaders must transform and armor themselves with sound ethics, creative/innovation/inquiry, and transformational learning that what my goals were for my family. If I were asked to write my life story, the one song I would select to be is "Lean on Me" by Bill Withers. When I listen to the lyrics of this song, my life story is a love for my family, friends, work, community, and going back to school. This song was chosen because I've always believed that I could fly, and the perspective in how I will support the family was able to lean on me, and nothing could stop me from my goals and objectives. Going back to school at my age was a top priority, and finishing school was my goal. When people see me, they know a person's full of life, excitement, freedom, and enjoys everyday life to the fullest. Individuals can be successful if they have dreams and hope to be all that they want to be, and that was they can lean on me. I love for individuals to see in my hope, love, and fun. I love working with people, cheerleading, dancing, acting, art, bowling, sewing, basketball, football, skating, sewing, and walking. I have a gold medal award-winning cheerleading team call the Silver Fox Cheerleaders, and the oldest is 82 years old. Now, to start this book, I like for you to know that each chapter will begin with an overview of the introduction.

Chapter 1 offered an introduction to the concept of my life experience from my perspectives, background, context, and history. Briefly discussed were the primary purpose, ingredient explanation, knowledge, family, thought(s) of today, and photos gallery. Chapter 2 focuses on the conceptual framework, ingredient explanation, experience, family, thought(s) of today, photos gallery, and the chapter's summary. Chapter 3 focuses on the creativity of the book. The chapter also concentrates on the ingredient explanation, experience, family, thought(s) of today, and photos gallery and the summary. Chapter 4 centers on the inquiry of the book and the results of the finding, ingredient explanation, experience, family, thought(s) of today, photos gallery, and summary. Chapter 5 will focus on the innovation of the book ingredient explanation, knowledge, family, thought(s) of today, and photos gallery and the summary.

CHAPTER 1

Ingredient 1 – An Ethical Educator

The authentic recipe in my journal has always consisted of family, religion, honesty, and education. From an early age, these were important to me. Growing up, I was taught to do as I was told the first time, never to speak when adults are in the room,  and immediately respond with "yes/no, Mama" and "yes/no, Sir." I was one of eight children, and my family's value was always to *obey my parents.* As far back as I can remember, my parents taught me that religion was of the utmost importance and that my vocational calling was my core value. I assess that I am hardly ever bored because I keep myself busy. Now, people know me as Dr. Blanche Penn, "On the Move."

My father instilled core family values in us all. My mother always told me, "Be nice to people, and they will be nice to you." Many years passed before it was my turn to travel the leadership road. One day, I decided to apply for the leadership academy. I learned a multitude of leadership skills, such as effectively communicating and working as a team player. Months after the leadership academy, I was forced to take a swift turn, learning about strengths and weaknesses. I decided to go down this new, straightforward road. Through the discovery of my leadership strengths and weaknesses, I found who I had become. It had a friend who encouraged me to apply for the position with the National Association for the Advancement of Colored People (NAACP) as the Second Vice President.

Even though I believe it was something I wanted to do, I almost did not apply. On the very last day, I filled out the application and waited anxiously for an answer. I got the position, and it was a new experience. I

experienced new things that changed my way of thinking. It has helped me to become more direct, open, and sincere, and has introduced me to new, attractive, and beautiful people. I have and will continue to make an impact on people I meet by being who I am: a person who uses the core values I learned from my family. My family consists of me, my four brothers, and my three sisters. I am lucky to have all of them still with me here in Charlotte, North Carolina. Since I have become an adult, my family has grown tremendously. I love these black and white pictures of my family. But over the years, I have noticed how my behavior has changed in the way I look at the world around me. As we know, life has risks and challenges. I can remember my family telling me to love your brothers and sisters, to do good things for your community,

and never do harmful things to anyone. My ethical perspective is always to develop a standard that would help me in my journey through life to teach my children to treat people fairly and work for what you wanted out of life. Right and wrong are determined to me by what you, as a person, know who you are what you think is the right thing to do in life. In working with diverse groups in my workplace, church, family, and home, it has become clear just how important it is to have an open line of communication. As a result, I have made some changes and now have a new perspective on life. The way I feel about my world is to live, learn, and be ready for any changes that will come my way.

However, setting goals and creating a plan for my career and future was essential to me. My critical thinking and problem-solving skills have improved as an adult learner. When I think about ethics and my values about how I want to raise my children, I do think about right and wrong. My children and I have an ethics code that we as a family live by, and that is to treat everyone with respect and do the right things to everyone that we come into contact with so that the world will be a better place to live.

It was vital for me to encourage my grandchildren to stay in school. However, I must share with my grandchildren to speak out when things are wrong in their schools. Also, my grandchildren were regular speakers at the school board meeting, city, and county meeting. I can remember when Anniah and her sister was speaking at the school board meeting and because of their comments was on the front page of the Charlotte Observer newspaper. Makayla and Destinee were a regular speaker at the school board meeting as well. Destinee has always been very articulate with words. Makayla once told me she was going to write the speech. It was clear they were having fun, and I loved it when they would call me, asking when I was going to the board to speak. It was clear what they were really after was going out to dinner, which we would do after each visit, and every so often, I would give them a little cash for helping me out. But I know that they had fun as well. My grandchildren are so special to me.

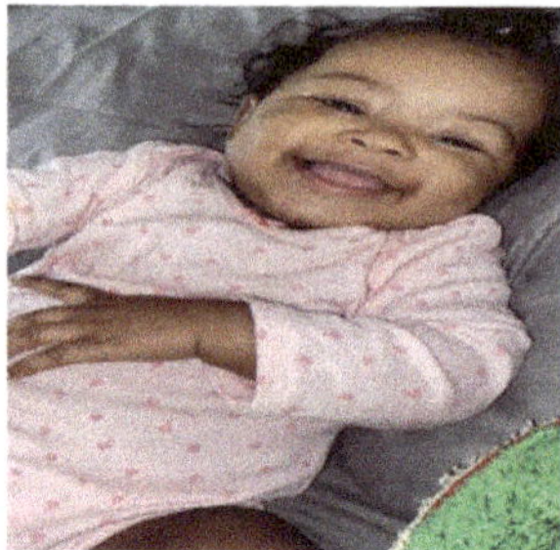

CMS shifts
pre-K debate
to the county

Sissy

Because my grandchildren are so special to me, I believe that reflection is powerful if you move forward with your life and let them see you doing well. It is not beneficial to live the way someone else wants you to live. Individuals must always protect their morals and values, and never let anyone comprise their integrity. When it comes to personal ethics

statements, everyone needs to do what is right in life. Personal development has been a continual process in my life as it is pertinent to my own, professional, social, and academic goals. I have received these gems of knowledge and added them to my curriculum vitae

under the authentic recipe for enhancing my interpersonal skills. The sequence of the ingredients in my recipe is essential because it challenges me to focus my energies in the most productive ways. My preparation begins with a layer of ethics analysis, then I steam in some transformational learning, and sauté creativity, innovation, and inquiry. The mixture of these ingredients is balanced to perfect the foundation for a lifelong educational leader. The best educators are the epitome of acquired harmonious balance both inside and outside the classroom. They are the nation's greatest assets and the reason why we have esteemed doctors, lawyers, Presidents, and other role models. Many teachers have sacrificed their lives for the sake of the students.

I can remember when I was a child, and teachers were the backbone of our community. As societal norms change, the scope of an educational leader's responsibility arises with more significant risks. Students are now dealing with educational inequality, bullying, obesity, and single parenting, to name a few. It is evident why educational leaders must transform and armor me with sound ethics, creativity, innovation, inquiry, and transformational learning for my success. I was in my twenties in this picture, the one in black I was cute then and still lovely today. Nevertheless, it was our parents and the community that kept us on the right track because everyone knows their neighbor. So, as you can see, my ethical values were working to be successful in life.

Ethical

My authentic recipe for educational leadership starts with an analysis of ethics, creativity, innovation, inquiry, and transformational learning. According to Mezirow (1991), "every educator has a set of limitations informed by culture and upbringing in their life" (p.1). I also have a set of limitations I have dealt with while volunteering at the school. One day, a teenage boy came to school wearing fake eyelashes. When I was a teenager, only women wore long, false eyelashes, and they were celebrities! Even though this was strange to me, I did not say anything to him. Ethics defines a balance of fostering diversity, encouraging students to aspire, and advocating for social justice. It is a choice people must make when determining how they choose to treat their physical bodies. God has given people free will so individuals can choose right from wrong and heal their body as a vessel, a sacred temple to be kept clean. Working toward a better, effective, and healthy way of living is one of the right choices that an individual can make for their life. After each school board city, county meeting, I would give them a *Though of Today*, everyone in the audience would clap or laugh. Also, after the meeting, they would share with me that I did an excellent job. I can remember when I was at the school board meeting talking about children been suspended from school. Here is one of the *Though for Today* that I would make up sometimes it made sense, and sometimes it did not, but the point was for them to listen. Read below:

Thought for Today: No One Will Pick Up

Thank you for calling. For English, please stay on the line. For Spanish, press one. If you are requesting an extension press their number:

- Press 1 to access your child on the street/suspended

- Press 2 to for job or college/ something you did call for that day

- Press 3 for jail-house operation, do you know the person you are calling?

- Press 4 to speak to a school board member, business committee, or parent support

- Press 5 to go back to 1 and get a hang-up

- Press 6 to speak to someone who cares

- Press 7 to repeat the menu

- Press 8 to please hold and never have an answer

- Press 9 if you know the person's phone number, please dial it now

- Press 10 if you would like us to call you back, please leave your name, thank you for calling

Nevertheless, I was involved in the schools as the President Council of PTA and participated in many school's PTA, and PTO, where I supported parents and students. Periodically, I like to share stories, concerns, and issues that affect our community. I visited the school board to discuss the needs of our children in our city. It became evident that many low-performance students were not receiving the support and materials they needed at their schools. In 2006, I began talking about the

Men Taking Children to School Initiative. I believe Dr. Gorman to have been the superintendent at the time. I met with him to discuss the program. I explained about Parent on the Move and Men Taking Children to School. Black Star Project in Chicago has a programmed called Parent University which we based Parent on the Move on.

I implored him to imagine the look on a mother's face when she knows she cannot feed her child as well as the look on a child's face when she sees her or her father. I told him that it was time to start working for all children. *"If today is not the day, then when"*? I am taking a stand, saying that the time had come for fathers to take a stand and be more involved in our schools. Finally, the Black Star Project, which was born in Chicago gave birth to Charlotte, North Carolina, to be the first one in North Carolina. After involving over 100 towns and cities in North and South Carolina in the program, we have parents actively walking their children to school. Nevertheless, I became the first person to receive the following Award from the School Board of Mecklenburg County promoting parental involvement in our schools. However, when it comes to the body, the temple should not be defiled. "Each of you must know how to control his/her body in a holy and honorable manner" (1 Thessalonians: 4:4, NIV). I wholeheartedly agree with this ethic.

Body

According to Willard (n.d.), "the human growth of the spiritual mind, body, and soul is in how I take care of my body" (p. 1). Many athletes take performance-enhancing drugs to have a well-shaped body and many individuals who go to the gym to get into shape. In reality, it takes hard work and dedication to get the desired results. People can damage the human body merely by eating and drinking the wrong things. When they watch what they put into their body, however, they can be healthier. Working toward a better, effective, and healthy way of living is one of the right choices that an individual can make for their life. If individuals have morals and values, wanting to do the right things, they can be successful. This was an award that I receive in the community with one of my best friends Delores.

Mind

"There are three fundamental attitudes which the life of the mind assumes about reality; judgment, action, and enjoyment" (Bonhoeffer 1995, p. 184). It is easy to assume the rationalizations of my mind have helped my judgment of going back to school and working hard on my courses as a senior citizen. It helps me to understand the flow of action of my studies. The mind is a part of my body that must work with all the other bodily functions. Therefore, an ethical framework is that I must have a positive relationship between my mind, body, and soul. When looking at the mind as part of the physical body, a harmonious alignment is created to function in day to day life. What a person sees through his/her eyes creates a mindset that life may not always be good or bad, that ethical values can change. It is critical that what feeds the minds is both pure and ethical, ensuring that people do not take for granted the gift of free will that God has given them as well as being positive contributions to society. As mentioned previously, it is not beneficial to live the way someone else wishes you to live. Individually, people must use their minds to open the morals and values of life in the way that my husband and I did in structured our family values.

This will aid them in finding purpose and helping others. As people understand their strengths and weaknesses, their mind is open to new ideas and judgment. When people looked at the rationalization of their relationship with their God, it helps them understand the flow of the mind. Through meditation, we can determine if we are doing what we have been called to do. The mind is a part of the body that works every day. If people have all their ethical values, mind, body, and soul, they will be in a better place to work for the good of the community schools, churches, and their families. "Be not conformed to this world but be ye transformed by the renewing of your mind, that ye may prove what that good is, and acceptable, and perfect, will of God" (Roman 12:2, King James). There is a famous quote student heard frequently from teachers,

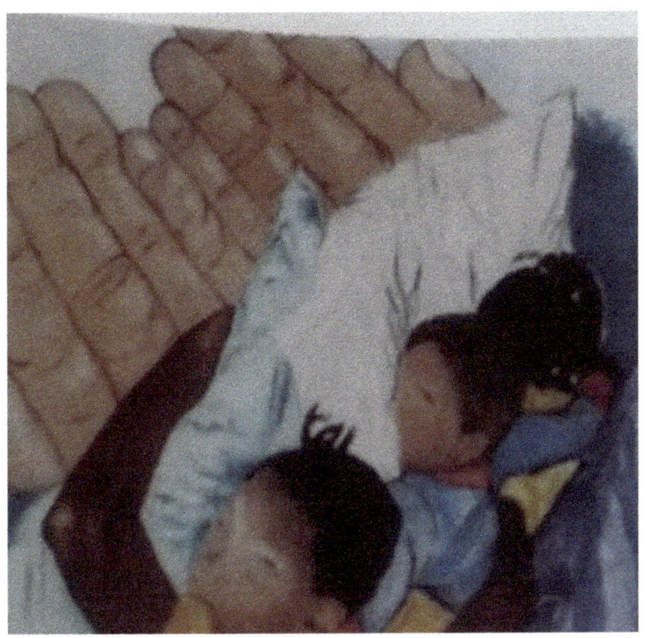

"a mind is a terrible thing to waste," Too often, students use up their energy and their minds by simply doing nothing. This is not beneficial to our lives and our bodies. Though our mind is extremely important, we cannot solely rely on it: *the mind is a part of our body which must work with all other bodily functions for us to think in a positive way about life.* If people were able to read each other's thoughts, it would not be a good example in determining what is good or bad for them. You must have all the ingredients.

Soul

Much like the mind and body, the soul needs to be aligned in harmony for people to function. "And the Lord God formed man out of the dust of the ground and breathed into his nostrils the breath of life and man became a living soul" (Genesis: 2:7, King James). Willard (2006) states that "almost everyone is acutely aware of how the incessant clamoring of their body defeats their intentions to 'be spiritual'" (p. 1). It has helped me to understand more about transformational leadership, and how the role of a leader can be different in my choice as an educator.

In implementing productive creativity, inquiry, and innovation ideas, it is essential to be able to understand these changes as a leader. According to Palmer (2004), "people have the power to choose right from wrong in their life" (p. 48). This process taps into my ability to become an active transformational learner, which is the second ingredient in my authentic recipe for educational leadership. This person is an educational leader and best-friend Judith.

CHAPTER 2

Ingredient 2– Transformational Leadership

Transformational Leadership

To achieve successful educational leadership, my authentic recipe must include a heavy dose of transformational learning. Cranston (1994) "emphasizes that transformative learning is rooted in the way human beings communicate" (p.1). Concerning this, Mezirow (1997) observes that "as an adult, it is the time that individuals learn to make their decision about life experiences and not rely on others to make those decisions" (p.5). After reading these quotes, critical thinking plays an integral part in making the right, sound decisions about one's life as an adult learner. Transformative learning gives adult learners this ability to think critically and autonomously. Deciding to pursue going back to school as an older adult was a hard decision. "Adults 'going back to school' were thought to be anxious and lacking in self-esteem based on their earlier childhood experiences in education" (Taylor 2012, p. 4). I did not want this to be my experience. My dream was to go back to school, finish with a master's, and later receive my doctorate. It was important because I wanted my children and my grandchildren to be proud of my accomplishments. Communicative learning plays an essential part in an individual's life through writing, plays, television, art, music, drama, and more. This type of knowledge allows adult learners to take place positively.

Communicative Learning

As I mentioned above, going back to school was important to me. "learning is a process that is learned through the world, unconsciously understanding your childhood, adulthood, and socialization of worldwide views, or events of this world that we live in today" (Mezirow 1992, p.33). Both experiences were beneficial and helpful for my transformational learning process as an adult. Holt (2010) says, "transformational learning is the process of recognizing, analyzing, and behave in certain ways" (p.2). Essentially, we need to unlearn to relearn. In many situations, one must adapt and overcome essential life lessons. "Teaching is an art, and it can be learned, but the major role of teachers is to teach and educate children" (Markie 1994, p. 86). As a teacher, you have to understand and acknowledge that you are responsible for the academic development of your learners. In my communicative learning, I can remember one example in the classroom where I was a substitute teacher. There was a disagreement between two teachers on how to discipline a student. This student in question was not following the directions, making one of the teachers to recommend suspension from school. The other teacher, however, did not want this for the child. After much debate, the teachers and principal decided to give the student in-school suspension. As a transformation leader, these teachers taught me how important it is for all children to be in a safe environment and that other students will adapt.

My best friend, Valerie, encouraged me to go back to school, saying you will simply adapt to the environment. She went on to tell me:

You can have your dream and know what it is, but you need to go back to school to earn the respect that you deserve. I will be with you if I am here because you will achieve it. Therefore, my suggestion is to write down of obtaining your four-year degree, frame it, and put it somewhere that you and everyone who comes to see you can see. Then, you have a constant reminder to keep going, even when the going gets tough, if I am here with you or not. Do it now.

After implementing her suggestion, I told her I did not want to go back to finish. Couldn't they just combine my two-year degree in Human Service and my two years degree in Business Administration into one, that will be a four-year degree? After I said that we both laughed, she told me, "No." She put a smile on my face, however. I kept going, getting my master's and a doctorate, and it has helped me in developing the process of discovering more about my leadership role as a student, citizen, and educator. Valerie C. Woodard always told me that I was a leader in our community, and now I am a leader for the good of my community. *Thank you, Valerie, I love you will all my heart. I feel that you are smiling at me. I know my husband, Felix, my mother, and Aunt Sarah are smiling, also.* These individuals were important in my life and husband, parent, aunt, and a county commissioner leader that live in our community.

Leadership Roles

When it comes to identifying assumptions in my leadership roles, especially when I first began to look at leadership, this example comes to mind. While reading over some homework, I made several assumptions that the information was worthwhile, helpful, meaningful, and beneficial to me in my learning stages. According to Mezirow (1991), "perspective transformation is the process of becoming critically aware of how and why our assumptions have come to constrain the way we perceive" (p. 167). Your decisions and actions will be different from what they once were, all because you learned something useful and applied it to your everyday life. Transformational learning, in conjunction with my leadership style, has opened my eyes to worldviews in a different fashion. Mezirow (1991), however, states that "not all learning is transformative" (p. 223). Learning keeps my mind, body, and soul open to new ideas as an educational learner. These are not always positive. During a triggering event, I experienced an emotional flashback, which caused me pain and natural emotion, my husband's death. These rings more than true. I have started my change implementation journey all over again without him. It was now time for my creativity, inquiry, and innovation ideas to begin working for me, helping me move forward and become successful. Upon reflection on the importance of moving forward, it was vital for me to work on different projects. However, everyone in one of the organizations focuses on collaborative solutions, and it became essential to define the problem that has occurred within our community. How were we going to come up with the best option for our community with so much violence? The challenge I found myself facing was the number of Charlotte killings of Black males. The most important part of my journey was going to be the next steps needed for implementation in our community.

The five elements described in the *Cycle of Excellence* by Hallowell (2011) are as follows:

- **Select:** Helping people get out of the wrong jobs and into ones where they can grow is extremely helpful.

- **Connect:** When managers work on helping individuals feel connected to the mission of the organization, the employees will be satisfied.

- **Play:** Managers should encourage imagination and creativity in the workplace.

- **Grapple and Grow:** When managers work towards positive environments in the workplace, employees will enjoy their jobs.
- **Shine:** When managers work with their staff, they will shine and be successful.

If we can see only through the eyes of a child, we would see life very differently. I merely want to share a short story of the violence with Black males in our city. I will never forget the too many who have died by the hands of officers. There are two violent crimes, however, that linger in my mind: Johnathan Ferrell and a college student both killed by officers. The police now believe Ferrell was seeking assistance after crashing his car. This was a case where I went to court with his family and listened. The outcome was not favorable for Johnathan Ferrell. Once again, the police officers got away with murdering one more Black male. When will we get tired of police officers killing our Black males all over the United States and around the world do BLACK LIVES MATTER to who only me and not everyone? I will never stop working on policies and procedures on why police officers need to kill so many Black males and see how they can put away some of their chemical weapons that kill many individuals. We wanted a positive outcome for the family, and after we left the courtroom, this is what we did.

I will never forget the moment when a friend called me and asked if my TV was on. I did not as I was doing homework and did not have the time. At my friend's request, I turned it on. Nevertheless, there was a second killing by a different police officer. A police officer had shot and killed Keith Lamont Scott on September 26, 2016. When I began to get close, an officer told me I was not able to go further. I informed him that my children were down there. He was friendly and allowed me to park and walk the rest of the way. My children called, asking if I was down there. Despite their protests, I told them that I was. They insisted I return home, but I would not. I did not leave until every child was off the street. That very night, I was on the phone, calling and asking where our community leaders and pastors were as I did not see any of them. Eventually, everyone began to arrive, wondering if it was me, they saw on the news or not. I continued to do this each night. On the second night, things got deadly once more. Justin Carr, the nephew of a dear friend, was killed. I spoke during his service as the family referred to me as Aunt Blanche. Below is a clipping from a news article featuring the fourth night in Charlotte on CNN. And in the newspaper, you will also see a comment that I made during the protest.

"ITS TIME TO BE LOUD. We are tired of people, especially the police, killing our black men," Blanche Penn, a longtime community activist, said at Wednesday evening's rally, where the mood had begun as resolute but peaceful. "Charlotte has always been quiet. But now, it's time to be loud." I must move on now. It is far too sad to think or write about in this book. Back to the present: it is 2020. I was born in the 50s, and I feel we are living in a new world, not understanding, and having too many questions for our future. I think we have a president who does not care about the people, so we must vote and tell everyone to do the same. So much has changed over the last few weeks in ways we could not have imagined. We are living in what is called a "new normal" and "social distancing."

Could we ever go back to how things were before COVID-19? I ask myself whether we would survive these mandated and confining conditions fifty-sixty years ago. And I wonder how we are doing today, years later. The answer to these questions is this: We must care enough to continue to stay safe by following the steps to prevent severe illness as outlined by the government and health officials. Now, in 2020, we are living in a time of the COVID-19 pandemic, and no one knows what will happen next, and the death of George Floyd, Jonathan Ferrall, Keith Scott, and the list goes on say their names. I will never forget the time I was thinking so much about life: whether we are going to be destroyed by water, fire, or storm. Yet here we are with a virus no one understands, everyone running around, unsure of what to do. What could be next for us? There are so many in the hospital, ICU, staying at home, police officers killing Black male and female, and not sure what is next. I can see that the world can get better for the future. However, you must want it for yourself. As always, we should be in this together. 2020 is a year that I would never want to come back to visit or live in, not sure of the future, but I hope it is nothing like 2020. We are, and I believe that God is in control.

CHAPTER 3

Ingredient 3 – Creativity

Creativity

Creativity, inquiry, and innovation are the third step into my authentic recipe. They have significant meaning to my leadership role in various ways as a learner. Creativity applies to me working in innovative programs that were designed for teens and seniors at the

recreation center. As a leader, creativity has helped toward my development of social skills in working with students. In this position, I am responsible for sports, extra-curricular activities, senior projects, ordering supplies, programming, part-time staff and volunteers, indoor/outdoor activities, budgeting, and overseeing the facility. I have found that it is always important to expand my opportunities for instigating change, using imagination and creativity. However, we will research a little about the cycles of excellence and how it can play in your life for success.

Cycles of Excellence

An encouraging place was one of the many creative ways my leadership stood out at the recreation center. According to Hallowell (2011), "play is good for business, and not being able to play hurts business" (p. 125). On the same page, he goes on to explain how play saved his life. As Hallowell tells his story, it becomes clear that whether he was a leader, doctor, or cook was not significant. What was vital for him was to discover that in a leadership role, one must do what is best for the situations, whatever that may be. While working in recreation for over thirty years, I have taken up such a leadership role. In this position, it became vital to build strong relationships with employees and to connect with them as individuals. I discovered that I enjoyed working with children in a playset because it was so much easier than working with adults. "If you cannot play at work, you lose your most valuable ability to contribute to work" (Hallowell 2011, p. 124). Working in the recreation center, I saw numerous children and adults who came every day to play games, work on their fitness, participate in hands-on projects, and create arts and crafts. Play is fun!

Play

Many years ago, recreation leaders participated in hands-on play with children. Nowadays, children are so absorbed in their technology, and it has become play for them. I don't believe this to be a good thing. As it saved Hallowell's Life, he mentions that "play can save your life" as well (p. 124). This is evident in a story about a patient save by a doctor who used play. This doctor received a patient and was forced to take action to save his life. By using games, dialoguing with the patient, and improvising, the doctor was able to keep the patient calm. Without it, the patient might not have survived. This demonstrates just how serious play can be to anyone, not only children. Fortunately, with my position, I played at the recreation center all the time, having so much fun. Life without play is a grinding, mechanical existence organized around doing the things necessary for survival. Playing can build your brain and stimulates the secretion of brain-derived neurotrophic factor" (Hallowell 2011, p. 124). Every time I participate in playing with children, I expect an outcome of fun and happiness. Encouraging playing to everyone, not just the children, is such a fun way to start your day. These cycles have helped me better understand my leadership role. As you have already seen, leadership is critical for me and has allowed me to reflect on everything

I need to be successful. "Learners must begin to transfer this new knowledge to create new behaviors and thoughts" (p. 8). Let's the review: Personal development is a continual process in life, pertinent to one's professional, social, and academic relationships. The ingredients for my authentic recipe in becoming successful leaders are as follows:

Ingredient 1: An ethical educator for moral values.

Ingredient 2: Transformational leadership for adult learning.

Ingredient 3: A mixture of creativity for originality, inquiry for analyzation, and innovation for improvement.

The ethical dreams I have developed over the years can be accomplished by reading to understand, listening to move forward, and holding on to hope to reach my goals for the future. I continue to remain focused on my dreams, being sure not to allow anything or anyone to distract me from obtaining my goals. Individuals have the choice to do right from wrong, understanding how to work hard by using the body, mind, and soul to accomplish their goals. These are a few pictures that have supported me over the years and family support.

However, one of my special supporter was Felix A. Penn, the love of my life, and now it is time to share with you a little about Felix and me because it is so important to have a passion for your family.

Now, this was when we were young in the 60th 70th, and I did look good, did I not? Fort Bragg, North Carolina.

July 26 was a beautiful day for Felix and me. My father Lacy and Darryl in the back.

Well, everyone in the community wanted to be at the wedding, so I let them celebrate with me.

Well, the wedding is over and guess what happens next? Our beautiful firstborn girl Petronila named after Felix's mother and her middle name after my mother. I believe that you should love the family that God gives you, and your parents might not be a star, might not be the President, but to you, a healthy parent. Nevertheless, we had three more children, Felix Jr., Jasmin, and Rafael. Love, your family, because that the ingredient to inquiry much success in your life.

<u>C H A P T E R 4</u>

43

Ingredient 4 – Inquiry Inquiry

If I Were Your Sister

I like to start this chapter off with something that was on my mind for many years. So, when you look at the word inquiry, what does it mean to you. Inquiry means a systematic investigation often of a matter of public interest. The student I chose for this case study is in the sixth grade. For this study, I have called her Jane. Now, Jane was a smart student. She had six siblings, all living in her mother and father's house. I decided to choose Jane after observing her frequent naps in the classroom and her difficulty in speaking with others. At first, I thought it might be an at-home issue since she was always asleep. After speaking with Jane's teacher, I learned this was not true. The teacher informed me that though Jane was incredibly smart, she was upset continuously due to a boy who was continually bullying and talking poorly about her. To avoid bullying, Jane would pretend to be asleep in the hopes he would not mess with her. When I asked the teacher why nothing had been done, she let me know that she only reports bullying if she sees it. I became concerned with Jane's

43

behavior and her struggles. Frequently, she would look at me and say, "*If I were your sister, would you want someone to do this to me?*"

Challenges / Existing Tension

Jane challenges were due to this bully, and her desire not to do any wrong. When she saw he was nearing, she would place her head on her desk. Although Jane complained to her teachers, nothing was being done, and no one was listening. It was clear to Jane that if she got into any trouble defending herself, she would be punished by both her parents and the school. She was especially worried about getting in trouble before a field trip, which her grandfather was paying a large sum of money. If she wanted to go on this trip, she had to be careful.

Action

In public schools, it is strictly forbidden for children to bully other children. Jane's frustration was not only by the bully but also by the lack of action on the part of the school. As she began to grow tired of him, she began to grow braver. One day, she turned to him and said: "You better be glad I am not like other kids that do bad things to others. My mother and father care about me, love me, so I do not care what you say." Can you guess what happened? If you were me, what would you do? *"If I were your sister."* What happened was that she became strong and was able to share with him good stories that made him turn his behavior around. It is so useful when other students can help other students to turn around their attitude and start respecting others. In this example, it was necessary to see one positive example that can turn anyone around if you stay focused on the goal, and she did. The impact of positive reinforcement in the school has dramatically affected on this student. Due to this, many participants have begun to inquire about our unique program on working with students that bully other students.

Nevertheless, for me, this is part of individuals working together and who feel part of a team, feel happier, and feel a stronger sense of belonging. However, after sharing that story, it was essential to share a story from one of my colleagues Mr. Keith Sturgill. Read his  statement below: Ms. Penn is one of our managers here at the recreation center, and she is known for "rallying the troops." Whenever there is an enormous task, she delegates responsibilities by our strengths and weaknesses. She knows what we are all capable of doing because she pays attention to our work. Then she acts by guiding us into a position where we all can be successful. She is one of the most strong-willed people I have ever met, with a heart of gold. She continues to work on becoming a better person, and she works tirelessly at it. She will set the bar and become a standard for everyone else involved. It is an honor to know Ms. Penn and a pleasure to work with her.

Nevertheless, I believe wholeheartedly that working with children at school, home, or doing something in the community to help others in their community would be successful for everyone. With that said, I understand that back in the late '50s, we didn't do a lot in our community. Some of our parents would tell us not to get involved in our community because we might get into trouble if we got in with the wrong people and politics. To clarify, I am currently involved in my community. I began getting involved after attending the Tuesday Morning Forum as well as NAACP, BPC, and various other organization meetings. It also helped that I had a business of my own, Winners Plus Inc.: The Voice 4 The People. In 2006, I started the Men Taking Children to School initiative. I ran for the District 3 School Board and District 106 House of Representatives.

Unfortunately, I did not win, but I had so much fun researching others. As a parent, I always have something to tell my children and the school board, county commission, my family, and the city council members. I will never forget one of my meetings with the city commissioners. There were only five residents from Lake Arbor, sharing their problems about the house in the city. After this, the tenants and The Voice 4 The People began fighting for tenant housing rights. It was necessary to make the commissioners understand several vital points while letting them know we were not going away until they listened. We were present for every meeting, discussing issues of affordable housing and tenants' rights. We did this for two years before they started listening to the residents! And it was a win for many of the Lake Arbor residents because we did not give up and, affordable housing is essential, and a place to come home was important for all those residents. After several of my speech, I would always give the city, county, school board members a word of *Thought for Today.* Keep in mind I went downtown to share information about housing, school issues, and anything important in our community is the reason why I did the thought for them to think about, so enjoy a few of my *Thought for Today.*

Thought for Today: What Are We Saying:

What are we saying when we sit at the table? Do we mean it when we say we want to help a child? Do we want to help a child when he/she goes to jail, or only when he/she gets a job or attends college? When words no longer have meaning, what will we say? When words are spoken and taken out of context, what are we saying? When a man needs help, will you pass him by? When he asks for change, what is your answer? When a child robs someone on the street, what do our words do? Do we have jobs to give our youths, or do we talk a good game? Do you mean to get children off the street with yet another band-aid program? Do parents even know what is happening in schools to help their children? Suddenly, the teacher is the only one teaching our children, and some only guide them to a test. Can we, as people, ever know what we are saying?

Thought for Today: Hold On

Hold on; most children are looking at you for the right school, good teachers, and a safe place to go to school. You glance at them, knowing they are neither your concern nor your child, so you keep moving. Children are always waiting for someone to care about them, to give a helping hand. In two words, you keep saying hold on. You tell the child, "Hold on, I am coming to help you," so that you can feel as though you are making a difference. But if that were your child, would you merely say hold on, or would you immediately give your help? Why do we say *hold on*?

Thought for Today- Thank you for calling

Thank you for calling. For English, press 1 or stay on the line. For Spanish, press 2.

- Press 1 for job or college
- Press 2 for jail (any time of the day)
- Press 3 for watch your words, speak loudly
- Press 4 for the Band-Aid Program, again
- Press 5 for PEP
- Press 6 for IEP
- Press 7 for Suspension
- Press 8 to return to the operator, please hold

Sticks and stones will break your bones, but words will hurt you more. One day, I called to get on question answered and the operator's response (not a live operator). Thank you for calling.

Thought for Today: 53 Second

Fifty-three seconds and still calling. Dial 704-000-0000. You must reach XXXX: currently, our office is closed. For Spanish, hold on. To access your account information, XXXX press 1. To report a lost or XXXX, press 2. If you know the person you are calling, you can dial it now or leave a message with the operator or her answer machine. Thanks for calling.

Thought for Today: Do not Close Your Eyes on Them – Displace Tenants Urge City Action at Lake Arbor

The following quote was seen in the newspaper, as so many of my quotes are, "At the end of the day, we need some help. And if you close your eyes again to displacement for our citizens in Charlotte, you close your eyes to the words you always say about affordable housing, so don't close your eyes on them."

Thought for Today: Comfort Zone-Speak

It is time for a change; we must step out of our comfort zone. As we journey through this year and last, we have had difficulties. We experienced mistakes, rights, and wrongs. We must no longer continue to look at Black and White only. Our world is changing, and we must step out of our comfort zone. I am no longer afraid to speak because my ancestors were free, and freedom is what I want. No longer should we stay in our comfort zone. The community, business, organization leaders, and people in our communities must work together for peace.

Thought for Today: Move Out My Way

I came to you today for the rights of all citizens in our community. No longer can I keep doing the same things in the same way. If it is not broken, some will fit in it, but sometimes, it needs to be broken to be improved. People say that it is alive, but not well, as we walk the street of Charlotte. Are you afraid? If we leave our home, do you think someone might rob your house? Can we find jobs for our youths? Can we talk to our teenagers? Can we pray with our teens? We cannot continue to do the same thing in the same way anymore. It is time to make a change, and if you do not want to change, *move out my way.*

Thought for Today: One More Time Mr. Story Man

One day, I went into the store, and I said Mr. Store Man I need that Mr. Store Man. And he said you need that he said, and I said yes. And I told Mr. Store Man he said yes, I said I need that there he said you need that there, I said yes. I told Mr. Store Man I need that their right there and he said you need that their right there and he said that their right there. Mr. Store Man Yes one more time. Mr. Store man I need that there one more time to Mr. Store Man, you said One More Time.

Thought for Today: Only a Dime

A man said to me, can you give me a dime. I said you only want a dime. He said yes, only a dime. I said, can you help me with this chair. And he said only the chair I said yes. And he said I cannot help with that chair. I said because you can help with that chair, only the dime will stay in that chair.

Thought for Today: We Can No Longer

We can no longer ride on the tails of our ancestors. We can no longer teach, not speaking the truth, because of our jobs. We can no longer sit in our comfortable chair with the remote in our hands. Changing when we have gang violence, low parent involvement in school, no jobs for our teens, people being evicted from their homes, displaced, and removed from the hotel, motel, and worse, their homes. We can no longer see or speak. We can continually be the same as if life still goes on. When will you listen to us? We are no longer able to talk without action and results.

I have noticed how my behavior has changed in the way that I look at the world around me. In conjunction with my leadership style, it has opened my eyes to worldviews in a different fashion. I know from working with individuals, I had to develop and establish trust within my community of leaders to be successful.

My quote during this time was, "If yesterday was today, and today was yesterday, what would tomorrow be? During this time, it was clear they hated to see me enter the meetings, knowing I was going to speak on these issues. I became known for the *Thought of the Day* and *Word of Knowledge*. I found myself on the front page of papers numerous times.

CHAPTER 5

Ingredient 5 – Innovation

Innovation

With a few stories in mind, let us return to my backstories. In 2006, I began working on the Key Father Initiative, Men taking children to school on the first day. With this, I was able to partner with The Black Star Project in Chicago. I will never forget working with the schools, particularly Newell Elementary, the first school to let us in their doors with this project for father and males. After the door was open, the first year, more schools came on board. I began working in West Charlotte, Turning Point, Zebulon B. Vance, Martin Middle School, and various other schools. The "Million Father March" consisted of twenty-five cities in North and South Carolina, and in many later years, over 100 cities and towards became involved with the march. Our Chief of Police, Monroe, and Harold Cogdell, an attorney of law, was among the fathers. Cogdell was the first person to support our children. Calvin McCullough was a volunteer, as was Charles. It was such a delight to see the children with broad smiles across their faces. It was clear that we had a responsibility to these children. It is my greatest wish that we, as a community, let these children walk through the front doors of employment, colleges, and not the back doors of jails. Also, I founded the Stay Focus Program, which mentored young boys at Martin Middle School and several projects at Turning Point School. For many years I was a former PTA/PTO President at Charlotte Mecklenburg School and served in a leadership role as the President Council of all schools in Charlotte Mecklenburg School.

Nevertheless, before all that happen, it was incredibly difficult at first; the organization and parents did not want me to be an officer. But many of the parents did not want me to have a position as an office but only bring the cookies and milk. They might be only for me, but that what happened to me. Later, however, I became the President of Vance High School when it first opened. After that, I moved on to Rocky River High School. Before my time at Vance and Rocky River High Schools, I forgot to tell you I became the President of the Council of Charlotte Mecklenburg School. However, it was like hell with some of the White parents who did not want me to have that position. I was continually being told what to do and how to run the organization.

Little by little, I began to get my hands wet and started researching more, and I start to speak out more for all parents. I informed many of the officers that we would get more parental involvement in PTA and PTO and not merely their friends to help them at the school. As I continued onto my second term, it became clear so of the White parents were trying to boost me from my seat, claiming I was doing way too much: they were not thrilled about my getting parents involved or how I spoke about the good, the bad, and the ugly. Nevertheless, by my third term, the goal was to vote me out, so I was uprooted because they did bring more parents to vote that day. That was when my children were in school, but I think PTA and PTO have got so much better but still need a little improvement because they always not involving all parents in their

schools. It was incredibly frustrating going through this, but I did it, and I am happy today to receive that experience to tell you about it. Now, one more story about my workplace for over thirty years with Park and Recreation Center. Because I was experiencing what I did and got a promotion, they did not like that I got the job and did not have a college degree. I could not understand why this was happening. Eventually, I came to realize that there is a vast array of attitudes, behaviors, and personalities, which can all change the atmosphere of a workplace for better or for worse. But I made it to retire from that job in 2017. As I am sure you can tell, this is quite a lot of work and responsibility in our community, but someone must do it. Over the years, I have been that person. With that said, I would like to return our attention to the story of my family. I would like to share short passages about my four children, Petronila, Felix, Jasmine, and Rafael, as well as something dedicated to all my grandchildren.

Innovation

Belonging to an organization that has promoted me to a leadership position has helped to make me an innovative leader. Innovative leaders are always beneficial to organizations, especially when they are trying to be successful because they have different styles that influence creative ideas. When you involved your children and grandchildren in your life, it aligned with many of my goals and objectives in life. My firstborn, Petronila, or Nen, as we call her, is gifted with so much talent and intelligence. She likes to tell me frequently how much she looks like her father and how she received her knowledge from him as well. When she does, I insist that she looks like both of us and gets both her talent and her intelligence from me as well. Petronila is a writer. She writes such beautiful poems and stories. I am excited for the time when she writes her book and collection of poems. As a child, she participated in beauty pageants and acted in a play called S.T.A.R. (Students Together Against Restlessness). She has three children and one grandchild. She is generous and kind, and so like me. She loves her family, always working to help them be successful in life while moving to the future with their goals. At one point, she facilitated a workshop on communication titled *Through the Eyes of a Child*. It was terrific. Now, what funny is I also give a *Thought for Today* to my children.

<u>*Thoughts for Today: I Wish You Would*</u>

My eldest daughter texts me, wishing me a Happy Mother's Day. Later, my sons and future daughter-in-law text me in turn. A text! That was all. Here is what I said to them: After texting me a question, I gave her a history lesson on her subjects. She did not want this, so she texted me again. At this point, I begin to become frustrated. I text all my children that if they wish to text me on Mother's Day, my birthday, or any other holiday for that matter, they must ensure there is cash involved! I told them that I would not text back for this reason: these types of texts are strictly for their friends. I am not their friend; I am their mother. Therefore, I believe I deserve more than a text. I stand by this to this day. When the next holiday arrived, guess what I received.

Felix

Felix is someone who can motivate the pants off a person thanks to his smooth speaking, and his eyes will make any woman fall in love with him. Felix, like his sister, was in the S.T.A.R. play, singing some of the songs. You should have seen the ladies clapping and  seen the ladies clapping and screaming for him when he threw a flower during such a song! Felix has facilitated several workshops with me at various schools as well. He is doing well and even has a significant other in his life who cares for and loves him. Felix is also on my Winners PLUS Inc. brochure. Felix always likes to look cool. Check him out. The S.T.A.R. plays with some of the members.

Jasmin – The Jazz One

Jasmin, at her core, is someone who likes to be different. She always has. And just by looking at her, you would not believe that she has eight children of her own. Jasmin has so much talent that you would not think that she can do hair, computer

skills, makeup, sew, and she has so many skills. In the play, S.T.A. R. Jasmin did most of the dancing training for the cast and a lot of the music. Jasmin has a beautiful voice, and she can come up with so many exciting activities for the actor, her children, and dance ideas for our dance team.

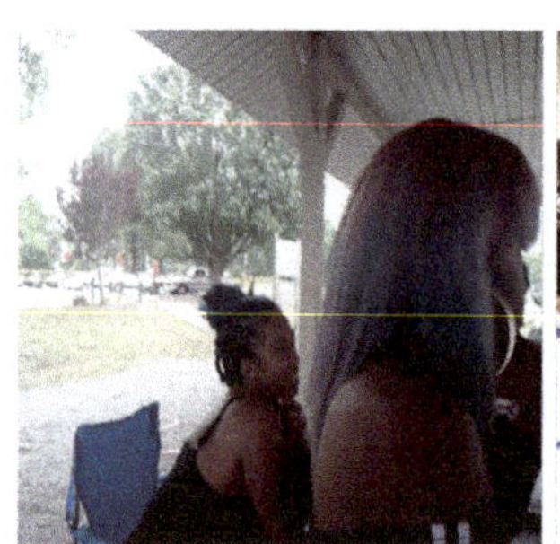

Rafael

Rafael has always moved on his own, and he is the type of person who comes around, and he is in and out forever on the Move. Like two of his siblings, he was also in S.T.A.R. as one of the main characters and sang several songs on stage. Like Petronila, he is also a fantastic writer, having written at least two songs in S.T.A.R. Rafael love to do video games, and he has so much talent, he can write plays and videos. One of his videos is Ruffle Winners had us down. His u- tube name is SuperStarRalph. Here is one of his videos. #SuperStarRalph #Youtuber #GamingYoutuber **RUFFLE WINNERS HAD US DOWN 19-0 AND THEN.**

Rafael is the student on the right in the back as a page in Raleigh, North Carolina.

All My Grandchildren

One of my grandsons, Malik, spoke about the Pull Up Project from Winners PLUS Inc. One of the commissioners was suggesting a fine for children wearing their pants too low. Malik ended up making the news thanks to his speech. One thing is for sure, the Penn name is always in the news with a story supporting the people in our community. It is also an easy feat for us to make the front-page news, the good news about helping others. Please, enjoy some photos of my grandchildren:

Annette's Post

PINK

charlotteobserver.com
The Charlotte Observer
EDUCATION
Just what the doctor ordered:
Encouragement for parents to read
to young children

I am the type of grandparent who always has something to say to my grandchildren. Sometimes, they inform me that what I say does not make sense. That, however, is not the necessary part. All I am trying to accomplish is getting them to think. To listen to my words and think about them for longer than they might normally. I would always tell my grandchildren and children, "because I said so." Do not lie, and I know you do it, too. More specifically, I use this phrase regarding how we communicate on the phone. They insist that they no longer need to call me; they can just text me. This is an issue, though, as I do not text well. My texting skills are so horrible that it is common for them to call me just to ask what I have written! (I have done this on purpose, please do not tell them!)

Thought for Today: I Told You Last Night, I Do Not Like Text. What Happened? You Texted Me Anyway)

Once again, I have received a text. CALL ME! I text back. I was in a meeting with my cheerleaders at the time, and we were discussing texts, calls, and emails. I remember distinctly telling them, "Call me. Do not text me." But here we are, a text. I sent me "call me" text but did not receive a reply. A second text came through, ignoring mine. I was getting angrier by the second. Now, a third. I text her again, "call me," but that does not work for her. Instead, I call her. She does not pick up the first time, but I call again. Finally, she answered and explained that I did not understand the long text. It was strange. While talking on the phone, I discovered her words to be much shorter. Finally, she got her answer, and I told her I would not respond to texting.

Nevertheless, I focus on our young people and seniors because they are our future and wisdom. I receive Award for the Champion for Children. Frontpage of the Charlotte Observer. Men Taking Children to School on the First Day.

Frontpage of the Charlotte Post and City Political- Men Taking Children to School on the First Day.

Blanche Penn on the front page of the Charlotte Observer when they close ten schools in Charlotte. And in 2019, they are working on opening back up some of the schools. Let me say one-word gentrification is terrible in our community.

Blanche Penn on the front page of the Charlotte Observer when ten schools were closed

In my city, there always something going on that I ask to go and talk at the city, county, or school board meeting with my friends Robin, Charles, and a leader from the circle. And now, COVID-19.

Silver Fox Cheerleaders. We do have a website
https://silverfoxcheerleaders.webs.com/. We are with our county
manager Dena.

Yes, not only was I a cheerleader, but I did anoint dancing for the Lord. My friend Felicia our dance instructor in March, 2020, went on to be with the Lord; she on the left. She started this dance team. Rest, my friend.

It was so funny that I had so much talent; I was a Barber, went to Cosmetology school, I was living in school, went to studies a few medical classes, law classes, but know I have a degree in education. My daughter and I did Tina Turner and Ike at an event at the center one year.

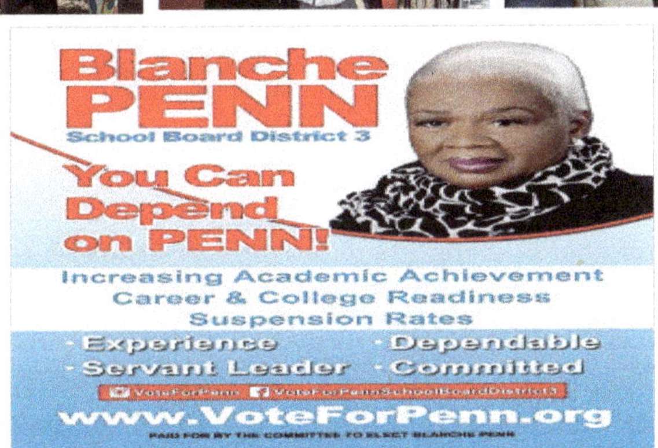

Blanche
PENN
School Board District 3
You Can
Depend
on PENN!
Increasing Academic Achievement
Career & College Readiness
Suspension Rates
• Experience   • Dependable
• Servant Leader • Committed
VoteForPenn   VoteForPennSchoolBoardDistrict3
www.VoteForPenn.org
PAID FOR BY THE COMMITTEE TO ELECT BLANCHE PENN

Funding

Some of our funding over the years came from Darry Johnson, along with Allstate, Fighting Back, ABC, and many individuals. Various other organizations gave to Winners PLUS Inc. and The Voice 4 The People.

Modeling

During my years, I have been a model for many fashion shows along with Mr. Man Fashion, Timmy Drayton, and Dianne Davis. I also hosted other designers and fashion companies. I have accomplished so much in my community, but believe it or not, and I was not sure I was doing anything! But let us move back to my love of fashion shows, modeling,

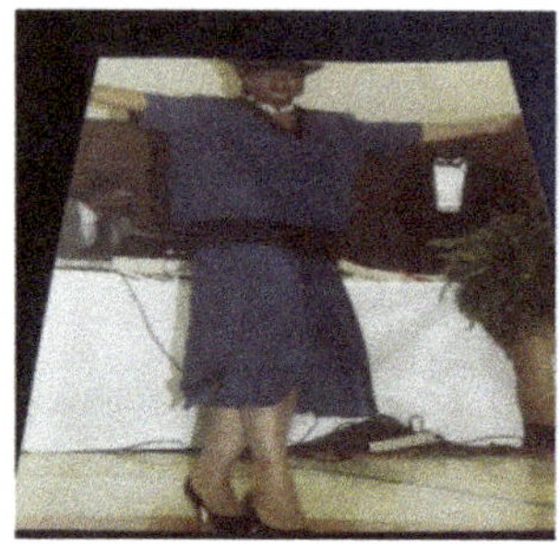

Kwanzaa

My journey goes on with a project I love Kwanzaa and telling stories. I was a storyteller for one year for both children and seniors.

Black History (Inventors)

I also work a lot with youth. Seniors teach them about Black inventors and the history of African American peoples.

I facilitated many Black history programs, setting up many inventors in the schools, recreation centers, and various other places. Apart from that, here is a link to one of our YouTube videos on the Black History Program.

EXIT
Mecklenburg County
Park and Recreation Commission

EXIT

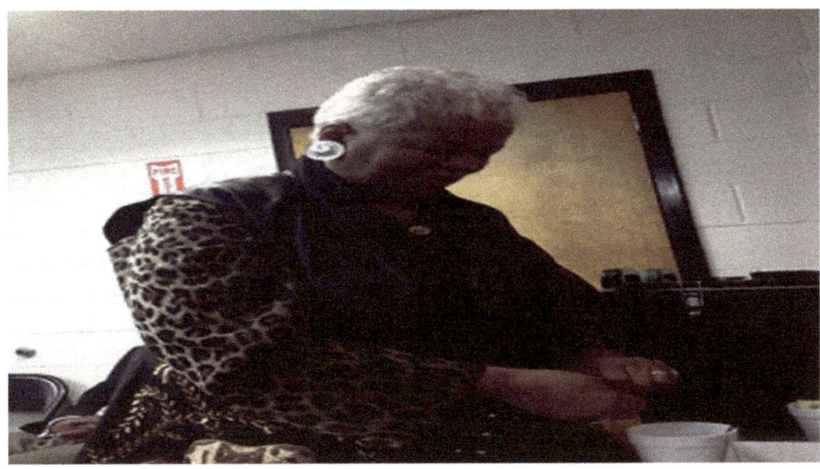

And now time for a coffee break.

I am almost at the end of this chapter, and things around were still moving fast. It is now 2020, and I was looking forward to walking down the aisle for my graduation in April of 2020 to receive my doctorate. Nevertheless, in March, I was on vacation with my best friend, and C-19 was in our cities, towns, and all the United States and Countries. But we still went on the trip and had fun. However, the world began to close around me. Stores, restaurants, schools, and then suddenly there was a Stay-at-Home order in place for North Carolina, across the globe even.

To tell this story correctly, I must start at the beginning. After receiving my doctorate, I suddenly found myself doing nothing but staying home and cleaning the house, not understanding everything going on in the world. My trip to attend my graduation was set on April 15, 2020, where I was going to be joined by Judith, one of my best friends. Judith would be coming from Dallas and was planning on meeting me in Portland. Unfortunately, everything was canceled thanks to a virus known as COVID-19. I am sure most of you already understand how heartbreaking this must have been. Countless students are going through the same thing. But to not be able to walk across that stage on April 25, 2020, at 4:00 pm, especially as a senior citizen, I was devastated. As horrible as this is, I will carry on. By the time this book is published, I will have walked down that aisle in full cap and gown either in my home, a hotel room, or anywhere that will have me. I will not be missing that moment.

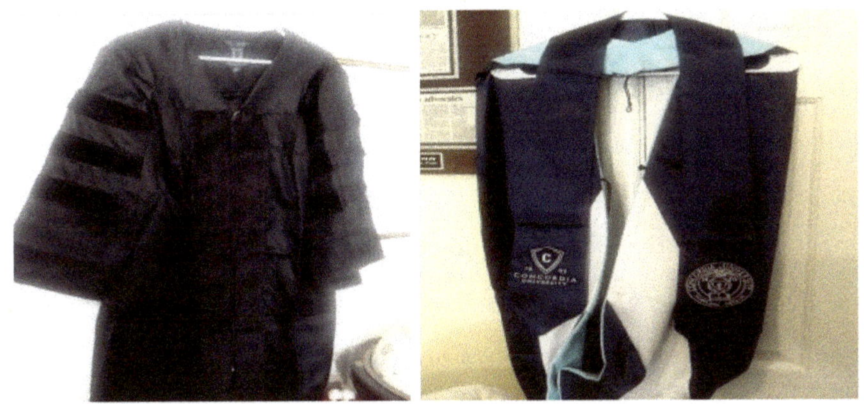

To fully grasp the devastation, I must provide you with some back story, sharing a timeline of events with you. As I mentioned before, I have thirteen grandchildren, one great-grandchild, and one on the way by the time I publish this book. It is so easy to talk about the bad and the ugly instead of the good, and I do not want to encourage them to do so. God will not let me. So, I will turn this book around here and talk about how many individual lives can be changed in the blink of an eye. My aunt was still with me before I began writing this book, but now, she is not. Once again, my life has turned upside down. I have lost my husband, my mother, my father, and many others these last several years. You can imagine the toll this can take on a person. One night, while sleeping, I had a dream which brought Felix back to me. We were sat in my car, and all I managed to do was complain and complain about everything negative in my life. When I stepped away for just a moment, he vanished. Not long after, he returned with one of our daughters. While he sat there saying nothing, she, too, complained and complained. All at once, he was gone, and I woke up.

This dream struck me to my core, making me wonder what I would do if God truly did bring him back to us. Would I love him, kiss him, or would I merely complain about the bad and the ugly as I had done in the dream? That night changed how I interact with people now. I no longer look at the negative. When someone comes to me with such negative words, I always reply with positive ones. I look at the world through different eyes, and I have realized how my action influence those of my family. Perhaps, if I bring positivity to the world, so will they. Peace and Blessing my friends and children. I hope you enjoy a little of my journey.

Note from the Author

Thank you so much for reading a little about me. There is so much more I would like to share with you but have not. This information, however, does give you a little information about the person I am today.

Dr. W. Blanche J. Penn

Appendix A

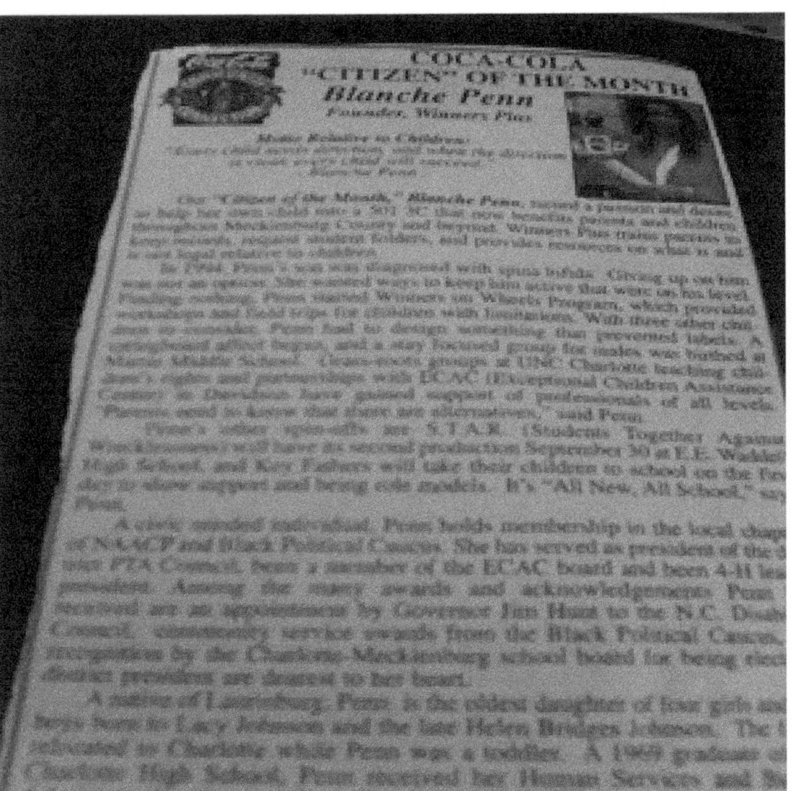

Appendix B

Summit's goal:
up, self-esteem

By Kristan Coley
THE CHARLOTTE POST

Pulling up pants can pull up a people.

The Black Political Caucus of Charlotte-Mecklenburg, Winners Plus Agency, and the Nation of Islam held a press conference Tuesday in efforts to publicize the Just Pull 'em Up Summit May 19 at Little Rock AME Zion Church.

This summit will focus on the negative appearance of black males that feed the stereotypical "thug look"

PHOTO/WADE NASH
...nche Penn, director of Winners Plus Agency, talks during a ...s conference Tuesday announcing formation of the Just Pull ...Up Summit May 19 at Little Rock AME Zion Church. The sum-...goal is to encourage dialogue between African Americans.

Appendix C

THIS IS YOUR COCA-COLA COMMUNITY CONNECTION CALENDAR...
Million Father March 2007
COCA-COLA REAL"

Appendix D

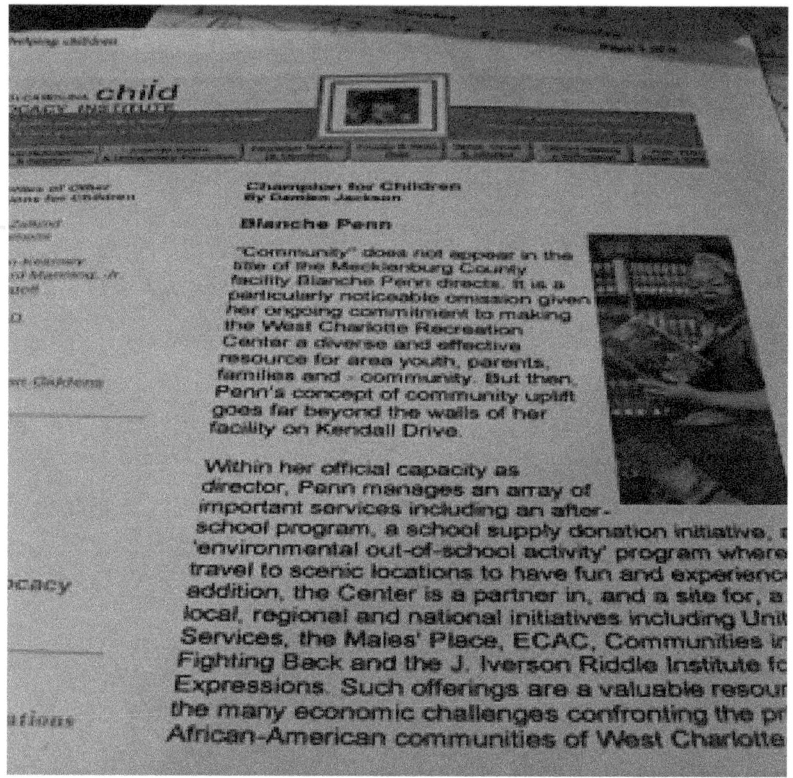

Champion for Children
By Damien Jackson

Blanche Penn

"Community" does not appear in the title of the Mecklenburg County facility Blanche Penn directs. It is a particularly noticeable omission given her ongoing commitment to making the West Charlotte Recreation Center a diverse and effective resource for area youth, parents, families and · community. But then, Penn's concept of community uplift goes far beyond the walls of her facility on Kendall Drive.

Within her official capacity as director, Penn manages an array of important services including an after-school program, a school supply donation initiative, environmental out-of-school activity' program where travel to scenic locations to have fun and experienc addition, the Center is a partner in, and a site for, a local, regional and national initiatives including Unit Services, the Males' Place, ECAC, Communities in Fighting Back and the J. Iverson Riddle Institute fo Expressions. Such offerings are a valuable resour the many economic challenges confronting the pr African-American communities of West Charlotte

Appendix E

Million Father March
I'M TAKING MY CHILDREN TO THE FIRST DAY OF SCHOOL
MILLION FATHER MARCH
www.winnersplusagency.org
Key Father
Winners PLUS Agency Inc.
For more information, please contact
Blanche Penn at 704-890-4201
Partnering with
United States
Census
2010

Appendix F

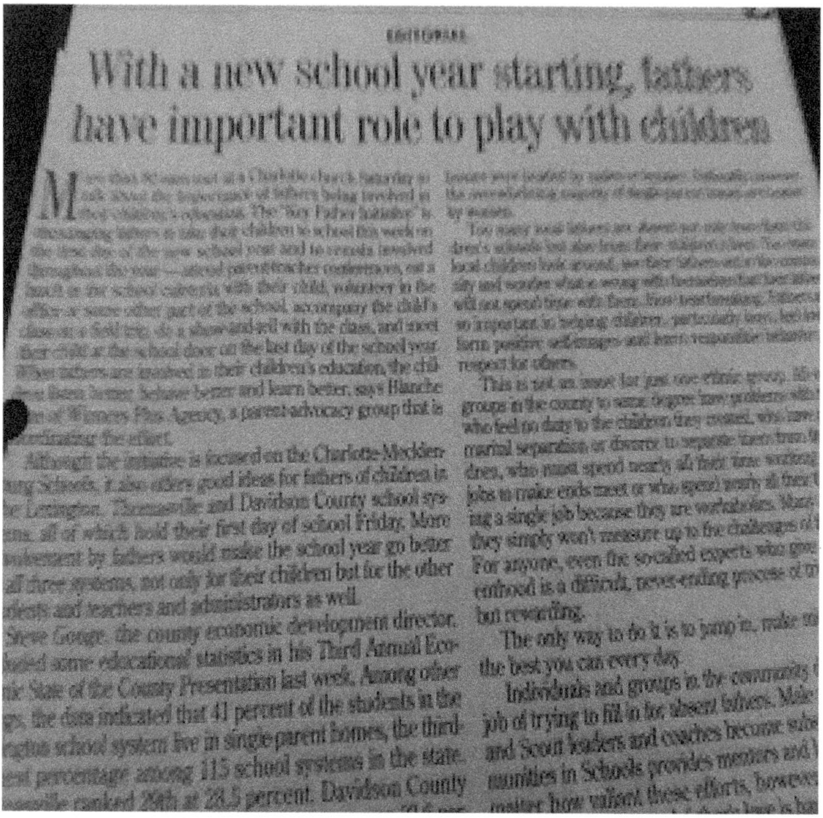

EDITORIAL

With a new school year starting, fathers have important role to play with children

[illegible] When fathers are involved in their children's education, the chil[illegible] behave better and learn better, says Blanche [illegible] of Winners Plus Agency, a parent-advocacy group that is [illegible] the effort.

Although the initiative is focused on the Charlotte-Mecklen[illegible] Schools, it also offers good ideas for fathers of children in the Lexington, Thomasville and Davidson County school sys[illegible], all of which hold their first day of school Friday. More [illegible] by fathers would make the school year go better [illegible] all three systems, not only for their children but for the other [illegible] and teachers and administrators as well.

Steve [illegible], the county economic development director, [illegible] some educational statistics in his Third Annual Eco[illegible] State of the County Presentation last week. Among other [illegible], the data indicated that 41 percent of the students in the [illegible] school system live in single-parent homes, the third-[illegible] percentage among 115 school systems in the state. [illegible] ranked 29th at 28.5 percent. Davidson County [illegible]

[illegible] respect for others.

This is not an issue for just one ethnic group. [illegible] groups in the county to some degree have problems with [illegible] who feel no duty to the children they created, who have [illegible] marital separation or divorce to separate them from [illegible] dren, who must spend nearly all their time working [illegible] jobs to make ends meet or who spend nearly all their [illegible] ing a single job because they are workaholics. [illegible] they simply won't measure up to the challenges of [illegible] For anyone, even the so-called experts who [illegible] enthood is a difficult, never-ending process of [illegible] but rewarding.

The only way to do it is to jump in, make [illegible] the best you can every day.

Individuals and groups in the community [illegible] job of trying to fill in for absent fathers. [illegible] and Scout leaders and coaches become [illegible] munities in Schools provides mentors and [illegible] matter how valiant these efforts, however, [illegible]

Appendix G

The Charlotte Observer
GENETIC HOT SPOT
Genetic
Scientists to search for families
in Charlotte with birth defects

Appendix H

CHARLOTTE PARENT
Who's MISSING in the Classroom?
Zero-Tolerance Enforcement Increases Suspensions
By Lelonya Moses

Blanche Penn thinks Charlotte-area parents may just have a "zero-tolerance" these days toward Charlotte-Mecklenburg's increase in school suspensions.

"I have four children, and at least once, every one of them has been suspended," said Penn, a Charlotte parent who now runs an alternative suspension program. "One was suspended for running, trying to get to his next class on time. They are not bad kids, and some of the things they were suspended for . . . were just stupid."

Appendix I

References

Bonhoeffer, D. (1955). *Ethics.* New York, NY: Macmillan Publishing Company.

Cranton, P. (1994). *Understanding and Promoting Transformative Learning*: A Guide for Educators of Adults. San Francisco, CA: Jossey-Bass.

Genesis 2:7. Then the LORD God formed a man from the dust. (n.d.). Retrieved from http://biblrhub.com/genesis/2-7.htm.

Hallowell, E.M. (2011). *Shine: Using brain science to get the best from your people.* Boston,

MA: Harvard Business Review Press.

Holt, C.S. (2010). *Mezirow's theory of transformational learning.* [Slide share Presentation]. Retrieved from http://www.slideshare.net/tsholt/mezirows-theory#

Markie, P. (1994). *A professor's duties: Ethical issues in college teaching.* Lanham, MD: Bowman & Littlefield Publishers, Inc.

Mezirow, J. (1991). *Transformative dimensions of adult learning.* San Francisco. CA: Jossey Bass.

Mezirow, J. (1997, Summer). Transformative learning: Theory to practice. *New directions for adult and continuing education.* Retrieved from https://cupo.blackboard.com/bbcswebdav/pid-232512-dt-content-cup/resources/week3/w3/w3%20w4%20 Transformative-Learning % 20 theory % 20 to % 20 Practice.pdf.

Nass, C. & Yen, C. (2012). *The man who lied to his laptop: What we can learn about ourselves from our machines.* New York, NY: Current.

Palmer, P. (2004). *A hidden wholeness: The journey toward an undivided life.* San Francisco, CA: Jossey-Bass.

Robinson, K. (2011). *Out of our minds: Learning to be creative.* West Sussex, UK: Capstone Publishing LTD.

Seyfarth, J. (2008). *Human resource leadership for effective schools.* (5th ed.). Boston: Allyn & Bacon

Sturghill, K. (2014), Trusted Professional Colleague, Charlotte, N.C. Interview

Taylor, E. (2012). *The handbook of transformative learning.* Wiley.

Thessalonians 4:4. That *each of you should learn to,* (n.d.), retrieved from http://biblehub.com/1_thessalonians/4-4.htm.

Willard, D. (n.d.). The human body and spiritual growth. In J. Wilhoit (Ed.), *Christian educator's handbook on spiritual formation.*

Retrieved from
http://www.dwillard.org/articles/artview.asp?artID=34.
94

Willard, D. (2006). *Personal soul care. The great omission.* San Francisco,
CA: HarperCollins.

Awards and Proclamations

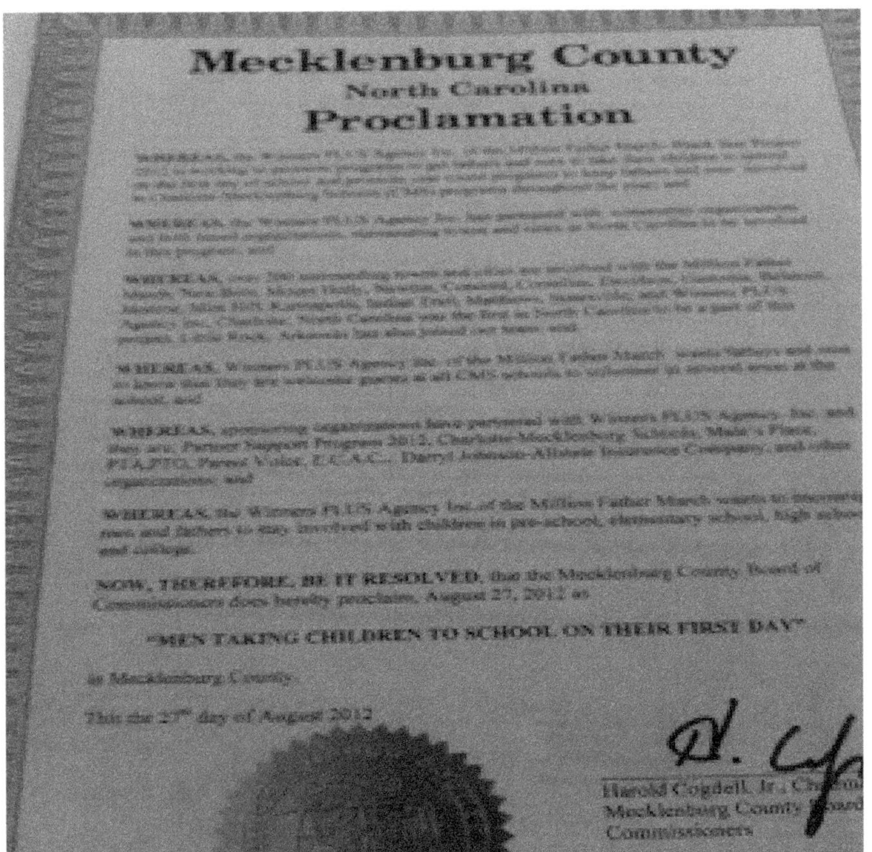

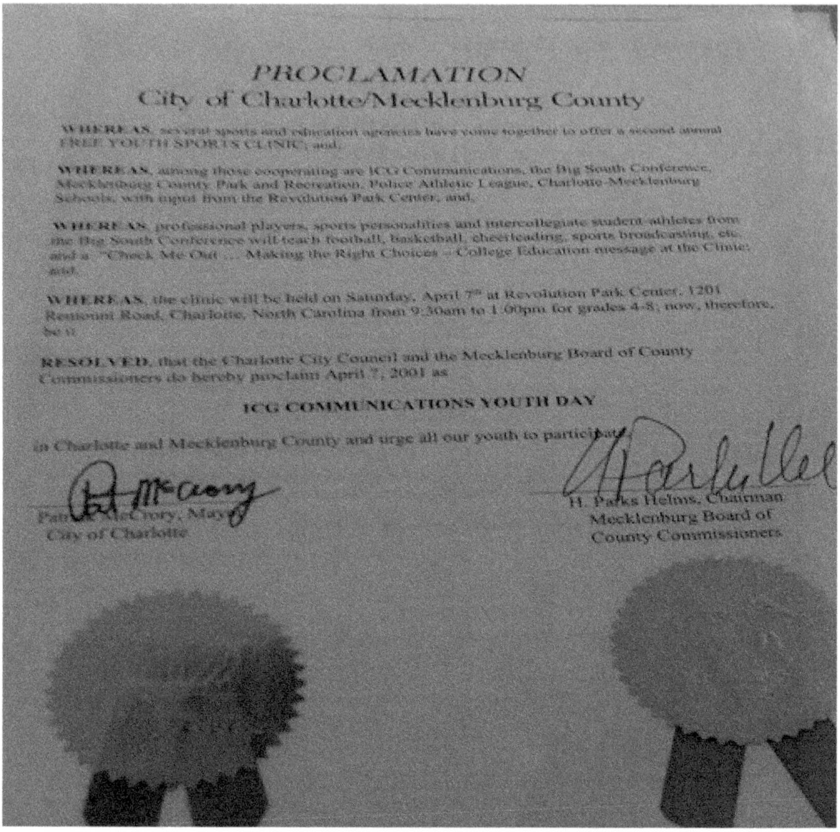

PROCLAMATION
City of Charlotte/Mecklenburg County

WHEREAS, several sports and education agencies have come together to offer a second annual FREE YOUTH SPORTS CLINIC; and,

WHEREAS, among those cooperating are ICG Communications, the Big South Conference, Mecklenburg County Park and Recreation, Police Athletic League, Charlotte-Mecklenburg Schools, with input from the Revolution Park Center; and,

WHEREAS, professional players, sports personalities and intercollegiate student-athletes from the Big South Conference will teach football, basketball, cheerleading, sports broadcasting, etc. and a "Check Me Out … Making the Right Choices – College Education message at the Clinic; and,

WHEREAS, the clinic will be held on Saturday, April 7th at Revolution Park Center, 1201 Remount Road, Charlotte, North Carolina from 9:30am to 1:00pm for grades 4-8; now, therefore, be it

RESOLVED, that the Charlotte City Council and the Mecklenburg Board of County Commissioners do hereby proclaim April 7, 2001 as

ICG COMMUNICATIONS YOUTH DAY

in Charlotte and Mecklenburg County and urge all our youth to participate.

Patrick McCrory, Mayor
City of Charlotte

H. Parks Helms, Chairman
Mecklenburg Board of
County Commissioners

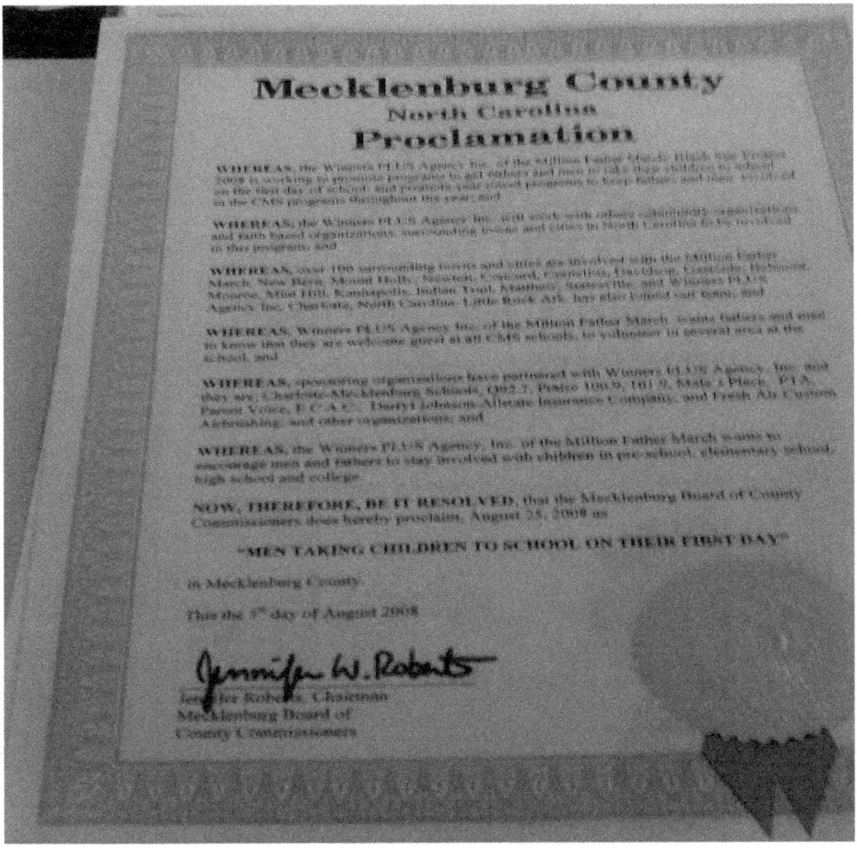

Mecklenburg County
North Carolina
Proclamation

WHEREAS, the Winners PLUS Agency Inc. of the Million Father March Black Boy Project 2008 is working to promote programs to get fathers and men to take their children to school on the first day of school, and promote year-round programs to keep fathers and men involved in the CMS programs throughout the year; and

WHEREAS, the Winners PLUS Agency Inc. will work with others community organizations and faith-based organizations, surrounding towns and cities in North Carolina to be involved in their programs; and

WHEREAS, over 100 surrounding towns and cities are involved with the Million Father March, New Bern, Mount Holly, Stanley, Concord, Cornelius, Davidson, Gastonia, Belmont, Monroe, Mint Hill, Kannapolis, Indian Trail, Matthews, Statesville, and Winners PLUS Agency Inc., Charlotte, North Carolina, Little Rock Ark. has also joined our team; and

WHEREAS, Winners PLUS Agency Inc. of the Million Father March wants fathers and men to know that they are welcome guest at all CMS schools, to volunteer in several area at the school; and

WHEREAS, sponsoring organizations have partnered with Winners PLUS Agency, Inc. and they are, Charlotte-Mecklenburg Schools, Q93.7, Praise 100.9, 101.9, Male-A-Place, PTA, Parent Voice, F.C.A.C., Darryl Johnson-Allstate Insurance Company, and Fresh Air Custom Airbrushing, and other organizations; and

WHEREAS, the Winners PLUS Agency, Inc. of the Million Father March wants to encourage men and fathers to stay involved with children in pre-school, elementary school, high school and college.

NOW, THEREFORE, BE IT RESOLVED, that the Mecklenburg Board of County Commissioners does hereby proclaim, August 25, 2008 as

"MEN TAKING CHILDREN TO SCHOOL ON THEIR FIRST DAY"

in Mecklenburg County.

This the 5th day of August 2008

Jennifer W. Roberts

Jennifer Roberts, Chairman
Mecklenburg Board of
County Commissioners

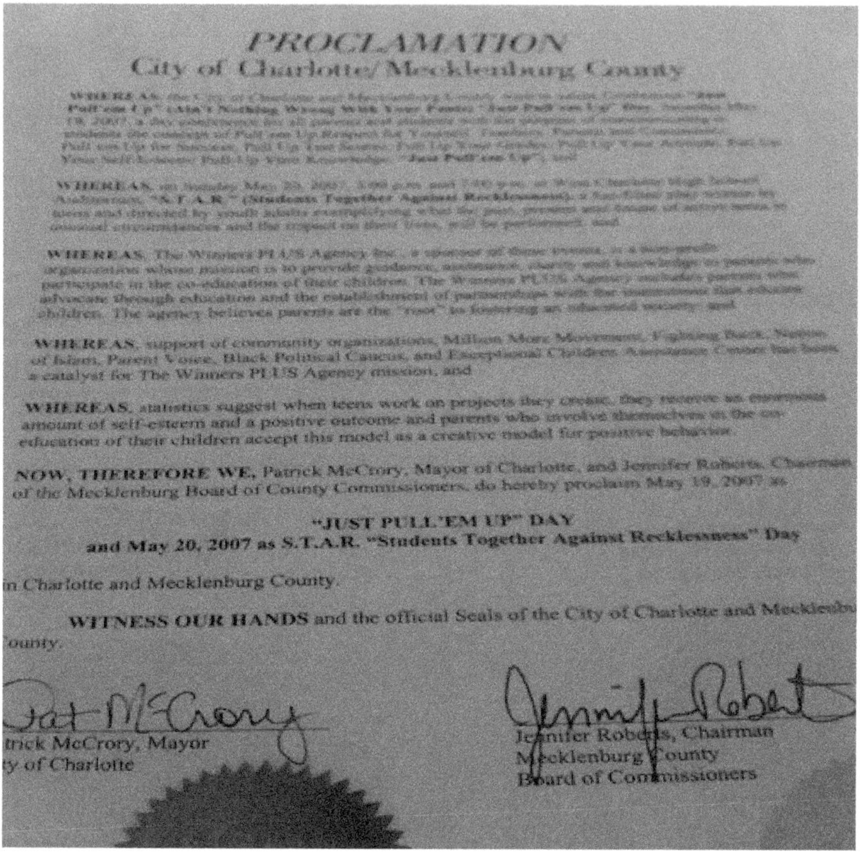

PROCLAMATION
City of Charlotte/Mecklenburg County

WHEREAS, the City of Charlotte and Mecklenburg County want to usher Conference "**Just Pull'em Up**" (**Ain't Nothing Wrong With Your Pants**) "Just Pull'em Up" Day, December May 19, 2007, a day conference for all parents and students with the purpose of communicating to students the concept of Pull'em Up Respect for Yourself, Freedom, Parents and Community; Pull'em Up for Success; Pull Up Your Grades; Pull Up Your Attitude; Pull Up Your Self-Esteem; Pull Up Your Knowledge, "**Just Pull'em Up**"; and

WHEREAS, on Sunday May 20, 2007, 3:00 p.m. and 5:00 p.m., at West Charlotte High School Auditorium, "**S.T.A.R.**" (**Students Together Against Recklessness**), a fun-filled play written by teens and directed by youth adults exemplifying what the past, present and future of reckless acts in criminal circumstances and the impact on their lives, will be performed; and

WHEREAS, The Winners PLUS Agency Inc., a sponsor of these events, is a non-profit organization whose mission is to provide guidance, assistance, charity and knowledge to parents who participate in the co-education of their children. The Winners PLUS Agency includes parents who advocate through education and the establishment of partnerships with the institutions that educate children. The agency believes parents are the "root" to fostering an educated society; and

WHEREAS, support of community organizations, Million More Movement, Fighting Back, Nation of Islam, Parent Voice, Black Political Caucus, and Exceptional Children Assistance Center has been a catalyst for The Winners PLUS Agency mission; and

WHEREAS, statistics suggest when teens work on projects they create, they receive an enormous amount of self-esteem and a positive outcome and parents who involve themselves in the co-education of their children accept this model as a creative model for positive behavior.

NOW, THEREFORE WE, Patrick McCrory, Mayor of Charlotte, and Jennifer Roberts, Chairman of the Mecklenburg Board of County Commissioners, do hereby proclaim May 19, 2007 as

"JUST PULL'EM UP" DAY
and May 20, 2007 as S.T.A.R. "Students Together Against Recklessness" Day

in Charlotte and Mecklenburg County.

WITNESS OUR HANDS and the official Seals of the City of Charlotte and Mecklenburg County.

Patrick McCrory, Mayor
City of Charlotte

Jennifer Roberts, Chairman
Mecklenburg County
Board of Commissioners

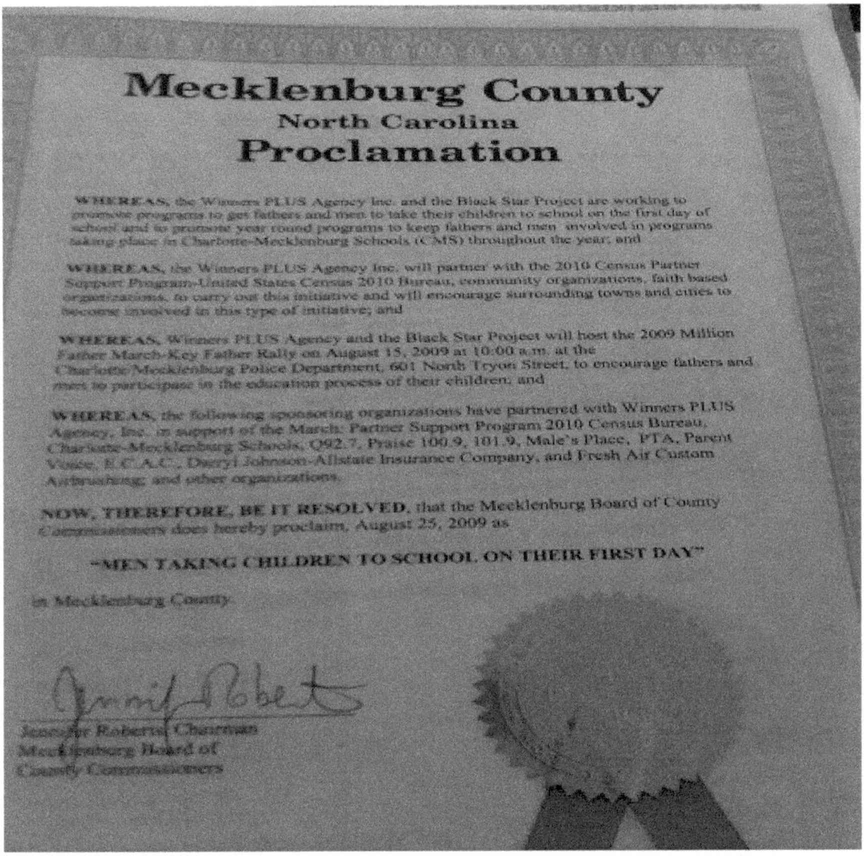

Mecklenburg County
North Carolina
Proclamation

WHEREAS, the Winners PLUS Agency Inc. and the Black Star Project are working to promote programs to get fathers and men to take their children to school on the first day of school and to promote year round programs to keep fathers and men involved in programs taking place in Charlotte-Mecklenburg Schools (CMS) throughout the year; and

WHEREAS, the Winners PLUS Agency Inc. will partner with the 2010 Census Partner Support Program-United States Census 2010 Bureau, community organizations, faith based organizations, to carry out this initiative and will encourage surrounding towns and cities to become involved in this type of initiative; and

WHEREAS, Winners PLUS Agency and the Black Star Project will host the 2009 Million Father March-Key Father Rally on August 15, 2009 at 10:00 a.m. at the Charlotte-Mecklenburg Police Department, 601 North Tryon Street, to encourage fathers and men to participate in the education process of their children; and

WHEREAS, the following sponsoring organizations have partnered with Winners PLUS Agency, Inc. in support of the March: Partner Support Program 2010 Census Bureau, Charlotte-Mecklenburg Schools, Q92.7, Praise 100.9, 101.9, Male's Place, PTA, Parent Voice, E.C.A.C., Darryl Johnson-Allstate Insurance Company, and Fresh Air Custom Airbrushing; and other organizations.

NOW, THEREFORE, BE IT RESOLVED, that the Mecklenburg Board of County Commissioners does hereby proclaim, August 25, 2009 as

"MEN TAKING CHILDREN TO SCHOOL ON THEIR FIRST DAY"

in Mecklenburg County.

Jennifer Roberts, Chairman
Mecklenburg Board of
County Commissioners

The City of Charlotte
Presents This

Certificate of Appreciation

To

Blanche Penn

In Grateful Appreciation for Outstanding Contributions to the Community. Whereas Such Deeds Deserve Public Acclaim and Recognition, Therefore Be It Resolved the City of Charlotte That This Certificate of Appreciation Be Conferred.

Dated This 24 Day of March,

Mayor
Charlotte, North Carolina

BLACK WOMEN'S CAUCUS
OF
CHARLOTTE-MECKLENBURG
33RD ANNUAL BLACKBERRY BRUNCH
&
AWARDS CELEBRATION
Senator Joyce Waddell, Vivian C. Spruill, Sarah Simons, Blanche Penn
Saturday, June 16, 2018
Theme: "The Time is Now"
Keynote Speaker: Bea Thompson
11:00 A.M. — 2 :00 P.M.
Friendship Missionary Baptist Church

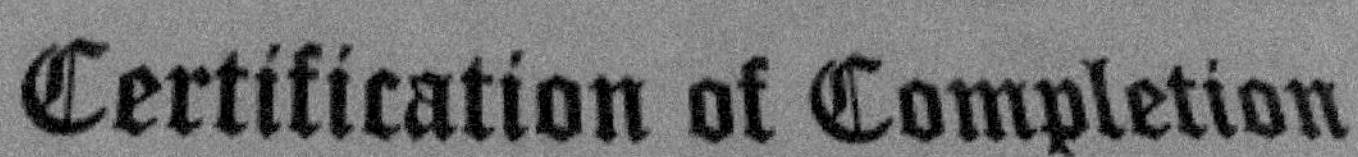

Certification of Completion
This acknowledges that
Winners PLUS, Inc.
Has successfully completed the
2018-2019 Out of School Time Professional Development
Awarded on: May 14th, 2019
Dr. Ross Danis, MeckEd President
Tatiana Brown, Charlotte NEXT Coordinator
Recognition on The Locator

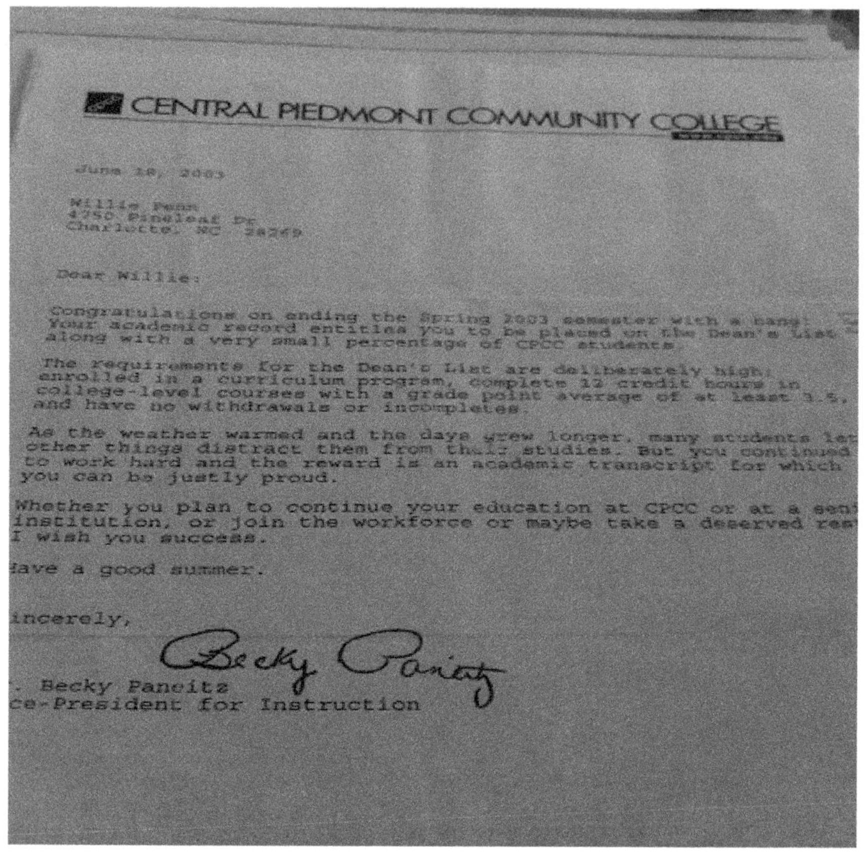

CENTRAL PIEDMONT COMMUNITY COLLEGE

June 18, 2003

Willie Penn
4750 Pineleaf Dr.
Charlotte, NC 28269

Dear Willie:

Congratulations on ending the Spring 2003 semester with a bang! Your academic record entitles you to be placed on the Dean's List along with a very small percentage of CPCC students.

The requirements for the Dean's List are deliberately high: enrolled in a curriculum program, complete 12 credit hours in college-level courses with a grade point average of at least 3.5, and have no withdrawals or incompletes.

As the weather warmed and the days grew longer, many students let other things distract them from their studies. But you continued to work hard and the reward is an academic transcript for which you can be justly proud.

Whether you plan to continue your education at CPCC or at a senior institution, or join the workforce or maybe take a deserved rest, I wish you success.

Have a good summer.

Sincerely,

Becky Paneitz
Vice-President for Instruction

Education

- University of North Carolina Charlotte Bachelor in Theatre (2013)

- Central Piedmont Community College Associates in Business Administration and Human

- Concordia University- master's degree- Education Leadership- (A- student- 4.0) (2015)

- Concordia University- Educational Leadership (A- 3.9) (2020)

- Brands College of Beauty Cosmetology License
- Barber College of Charlotte Barber License

Services

- Champion for Children- Awards by North Carolina- Raleigh, NC
- Governor Hunt Appointment- North Carolina Disability Council
- National Recreation and Park Association- 25 years or more

Professional Experience

- Facility Manager 1 (West Charlotte Recreation Center- 6 years)
- Recreation Specialist
- Assistant Librarian Central Piedmont Community College

Professional Organizations and Civil Affiliations

- Member, Leadership Academy, Mecklenburg County Park, and Recreation
- Member, Alpha Phi Chi, Chair of the Torchlight
- Member, Black Political Caucus, Membership Chair
- Member, Black Women Caucus, Chaplain
- 2nd Vice President, National Advancement for Colored People, NAACP
- PTA Council President 2000- 2002, 2004

- PTA President, Vance High School

- Parent Leadership, Lee Institute

- Board Members, Charter School

- Board Commission- Park and Recreation

- Winners PLUS Agency, Inc. Executive Director, non-profit, www.winnersplusagencu.org

- -Parent on the Move Workshops for parents and students

Awards and Honors

- Mug Award for organizing special senior programs at park and recreation

- The Revolution Neighborhood Association Award for the Employee of the Year

- NAACP Awards Unsung Hero

- Awards Glider Track Team for Community Services

- Award North Carolina Raleigh Community Service (more awards)

CPSIA information can be obtained
at www.ICGtesting.com
Printed in the USA
BVHW062055201020
591388BV00001B/1